surrender:
a Christian's guide
to dependence

surrender

Surrender:

A Christian's Guide to Dependence

by Michael Summers Jr.

Front cover image by Mike Wilson at unsplash.com
Front cover created on canva.com

ISBN-10: 1532764618
ISBN-13: 978-1532764615

DEDICATION

This book is dedicated to the students at Countryside.
Your love for Christ and your growing hunger for His
Word motivated my heart to shepherd you in this way.
I love you.

surrender

CONTENTS

introduction   11

1 - astray   15

2 – breaking point   27

3 – the art of surrender   37

4 – under new management   47

5 – the war on independence   57

6 – a warning   67

closing thoughts   75

THANK YOU

I want to thank Pastor Scott Nicoll for being a constant mentor, brother and hero in my life. You are my Paul. You are the reason I fell in love with student ministry.

I want to especially thank my gorgeous wife, Kimberly. You beautifully and willingly endured more responsibility in our home to enable the fulfillment of this project. Thank you for graciously gifting me with the space and time needed to complete this book. May you be presented with a special reward in the Kingdom for your selfless and difficult sacrifice. Your heart reminds me of Jesus.

Thank you, Laura Knott, for your patient and generous spirit in the edit process. You were kind in spite of my juvenile usage of English grammar and punctuation. Thanks for making this a real book.

surrender

introduction

Have you ever had something stolen from you? Even worse, have you ever had something stolen that had your name on it? I admit, I used to be the king of doing that. I "borrowed" labeled things from my friends and roommates with a permanent timeframe— or at least until I would get caught. Over time God has helped me grow in this area, but He has also allowed it to turn around and happen to me repeatedly.

There is an ongoing feud with one of my brothers and a few friends. In high school I bought a t-shirt from a discount department store. I clearly remember this along with the other items I purchased. That t-shirt somehow made its way to a friend's house where he wore it for two years. It then taken by another friend who had it for two years. Now my younger brother has it and has worn it for at least eight years. Here's the strange part: each of the three guys claim that they bought the shirt! As you can imagine, when I try to convince them that I bought it, I get laughed at and the argument continues. Something that I paid for is being claimed by others.

That's a slightly gross, but clear picture of a deeper truth. The truth is that we often claim to own what rightfully belongs to God: *our lives*. When you and I live as the "rightful owners" of our lives, the result is disobedience to God. That is what this book is about. It is about forsaking the mindset of self-ownership in order to submit to the ownership and authority of Jesus.

I want to challenge you to spend some time evaluating your life as we go through each of these chapters. My prayer is that God would use this book as a tool to explain your need for surrender as well as how it can happen in your life. The goal is to point you to a deeper dependence and satisfaction found only in our King. This will be found when you and I surrender complete ownership of our hearts back to God.

You know, if my brother surrendered that t-shirt back to me after all these years, I would say "Gross!" and would probably not wear it. Seriously, it has been worn by three other guys for the past twelve years! Surrender is not like that with God. When you and I surrender our lives back to God's ownership, He doesn't say "Gross!" but instead offers forgiveness, purpose and joy. It is such a wonderful thing to be owned by Him!

I trust that this book will be a helpful guide against the theft that you and I are guilty of committing towards God. Take a moment to seek His help in prayer as you begin the first chapter.

1 - astray

*"All we like sheep have gone astray;
we have turned—every one—to his own way;
and the Lord has laid on Him the iniquity of us all."*
Isaiah 53:6

DANGEROUS ADVICE

I remember riding in the car with some friends. I was nearing the end of high school and in the midst of making some very important future decisions. The car ride was long and the conversation turned to my plans for college, career interests, etc. Like most high school seniors, I was interested in a variety of pursuits. Even though I had many ideas and possibilities before me, in the back of my mind, I already knew where God was calling me. I knew God was calling me to a life of Christian service in ministry. The problem was that a selfish piece of my heart sometimes wanted a different path than God's calling. It was that selfish part of my heart that did not *love* what He was calling me to do.

As we discussed different options on this car ride, I clearly remember the advice of one of the individuals. They said, "You just need to follow your heart." I liked that advice. It sounded good. It sounded fulfilling. If I were to follow my heart, I could pursue doing the things that I loved and the things that interested me most. That advice seemed wise. In fact, everyone in the car agreed it was good, and I remember the driver nodding in approval. But the truth is that the instruction to "follow your heart" was the most dangerous advice I have ever been given. Here's why:

"All we like sheep have gone astray; we have turned—every one—to his own way…" (Is. 53:6a).

This verse reveals an important truth about us. It teaches us that "our own way," that is, the way we want to go when we follow our hearts, takes us "astray." Astray from what? Astray from God's way. This tells us something: a piece of our hearts craves independence. Somewhere in our hearts there is a natural desire to live our way instead of God's way. Our hearts like going "astray" because we like being pioneers of our future. Independence is important to us. It appeals to us. That is why commercials will say things like "Have it *your way.*" Everyone wants to be able to live in such a way that they don't need anyone else. You and I are familiar with this. I have already seen it in my 4-year-old son. He doesn't like me to buckle him into his car seat—he wants to do it all by himself. That mindset just multiplies as we grow older. We don't like to ask for help. Even worse, we really don't like to do things someone else's way. It's not just cheeseburgers that we want our way, we want to *live and function* our way. This is natural. This is built in. Everyone wants to be an independent thinker, independently wealthy, the creators of our own destiny. On the flip side, we don't have a natural craving to be dependent. Our ideas about a fulfilling life typically don't include goals of servanthood. It's against our nature. Why is that? Here's a clue from Genesis 3.

"So when the woman saw that the tree was good for food, and that it was a delight to the eyes, and that the tree was to be desired to make one wise, she took of its fruit and ate, and she also gave some to her husband who was with her, and he ate" (Gen. 3:6).

CRAVING INDEPENDENCE

What enticed Eve the most was independence from God.

- She "saw that the tree was good for food." Regardless of God's forbiddance, Eve found a purpose for the fruit (independence from God's purpose).

- She saw "it was a delight to the eyes." Regardless of God's forbiddance, Eve found a pleasure in the fruit (independence from God's pleasures).

- She saw "that the tree was desired to make one wise." Regardless of God's forbiddance, Eve found wisdom to be received from the fruit (independence from God's wisdom).

You see, it was independence that Satan was after with Eve. Satan wanted God's highest creation on the earth to revolt against the Creator. If this could happen, it would ruin the original purpose of God (all of creation bringing glory and praise to Himself forever). If Satan could trick created beings into seeking their own purpose, it would be his greatest attack against God. We all know the story. Satan's plan worked. After Adam and Eve chose independence, man has been born with a consuming desire for his own glory. Since then, every human being after Adam and Eve has been born with that sin nature—a nature that craves to be independent from God.

You and I can relate to that. Think about a time when you've made a bad choice or did something you knew was wrong. You can probably remember a strong urge to do what you wanted. Have you ever had that urge? Have you ever been faced with a decision to obey or to sin and ended up sinning because it was what you wanted? Our personal history is living proof that something inside craves independence from God. It shows up when we face the decision to obey or disobey and feel that urge…the urge to do and live and follow what we want.

So why was the advice to "follow your heart" such bad advice? Simple. My heart is not safe. If I follow my heart there is something inside that will only lead me (1) away from God's purposes, (2) away from God's pleasures, and (3) away from God's wisdom. This is what the "astray way" is.

THE ASTRAY WAY

Perhaps you agree with most of this so far. You can see that we already have selfish desires within our human nature. That is not too difficult to recognize. Still, there are many people who agree with these things and have this knowledge, but continue in a life pattern of going astray. This is because, although the knowledge is there, a *belief* still exists that the "astray way" is not a bad choice. When someone chooses to follow the selfish desires of the heart, they really do not have a problem with the "astray way." In fact, it seems to be the right way. Scripture has something to say about this:

"There is a way that seems right to a man, but its end is the way to death" (Prov. 16:25).

That is a pretty strong statement. The "astray way" is the way to death? By no means does this verse communicate that you will be killed instantly for disobeying God. It does not mean you will walk outside and get hit by a truck if you go your own way in life. Rather, it speaks of an eventual ongoing killing. We will see that in a moment. This is not at all referring to a physical death, but a spiritual death. Spiritual death is much different than your heart stopping. It is different than simply an end to your life. The truth is, spiritual death is *far worse* than physical death.

"And do not fear those who kill the body but cannot kill the soul. Rather fear him who can destroy both soul and body in hell" (Matt. 10:28).

Spiritual death is not an end. It is an ongoing horrific peril that *never* ends. This is different than our usual concept of death. We often see death as an end to something, not an ongoing experience. However, spiritual death is a very real, unimaginable, constant torment. It is a destroying of both your body and soul that never stops being destroyed. This is hard to comprehend, but this is where the "astray way" leads. It leads to Hell.

There are three major things (among so many others) that make Hell and spiritual death the worst possible experience in all existence.

1. God's *grace* is not in Hell. All people in this life experience God's "common grace." This is the grace of God seen in things like health, sunshine and rain, protection, conveniences and enjoyment of life. This means that going astray and seeking independence from God finally reaches a horrifying destination. The grace of God that blesses, protects, gives mercy, provides rest, establishes peace and produces joy has been removed. When you finally reach a destination where there is no more common grace, what do you have? You have nothing good left in your existence: no blessing, no protection, no mercy, no rest, no peace, no joy. Why? Because all of those things are experienced only through the grace of God. Amazingly, some people are ok with that. But they don't realize what else is in Hell.

2. Hell is a place of *punishment*. This is a brand new experience for any human. When a person enters into Hell, for the first time they experience God's wrath and anger. This gets way more terrifying when you understand that God is the Supreme Being of the universe, and His wrath and anger are infinitely unbearable. God's punishment is worse than anything that exists in this universe. There is nothing that compares to it. There is fire that burns the body, worms that never stop eating the body

while it burns and never one second of relief. There is no relief, because God's grace is not there protecting, giving mercy, giving rest, giving peace. There is no way out. Literally there is no safe place, nowhere to run, and no relief from the pain. That's not all.

3. Hell is a place of total *darkness*. Never again will the person who enters be able to see again. It's the darkest of all darkness. Oh, and in that darkness, you are alone. That means no one sees anyone else. No one gets to hang out and chat with buddies who make it there. Instead there is the loud screams of others experiencing the same unbearable punishment mixed in with a person's own screaming.

This is where the "astray way" leads. At the end of the path is a drop off into the most unimaginable horror of being constantly destroyed without end. Sadly, many people are running down this path. People are even cheering *for* the people running down this path! The way of independence may be celebrated, but it is the way to death. So the advice to "follow your heart" is the most dangerous advice of all. It is the sweet-smelling, candy-coated path leading to a place where God's grace is removed—a place where His wrath and anger are relentlessly crushing bodies and souls who refused to follow Him. Every human being is born already running down this path.

What about Christians? What about those who do know Jesus, but have struggled and sought to go back to the "astray way"? Here are three quick things the "astray way" provides for believers.

1. It provides *emptiness*. One time a friend showed me a Tootsie Roll flavored chap stick. Like any normal person I took a bite. (Ok, I'm not normal.) I knew it wasn't a real Tootsie Roll, but it smelled great! I'll never forget that nasty wax in my mouth. In a similar way, a believer knows deep in his heart that turning away from God isn't going to be satisfying long-term…but it looks so good! The result is that the desire to be happy and the craving to be fulfilled ends up not being satisfied. Turning away from real, deep satisfaction in God to pursue lesser satisfaction is like eating chap stick hoping it tastes better than a Tootsie Roll. Everything that seemed to look good ends up tasting like nasty wax.

2. It provides *loneliness*. Sometimes I wrestle with my kids in my bed. They love it. Every once in a while my 2-year-old daughter pulls a blanket over her head and can't find her way out. She usually starts crying and calling out "Daddy!" because she cannot see me, even though I haven't moved the

entire time. She feels helpless and alone. The reason is because she has trapped herself. The "astray way" is like that for a Christian. God has not left or forsaken us. But when we choose independence, it is like pulling a blanket over our lives. We are unable to feel His presence and we feel utterly alone. This means that the peace and security we had in His presence is no longer felt or experienced.

3. It provides *misery and regret*. When we reject God, He allows us to run away and experience the emptiness and loneliness of doing life all by ourselves. The more we seek fulfillment our way, the more miserable we eventually become. We eventually reach a point where we realize that our time has been wasted and we have failed to fulfill God's intended purpose for our lives. Then comes the heaviness of regret.

Without God, you and I are hopeless beings. We can't find fulfillment. We can't always protect ourselves. We can't meet the deep needs and desires of our own hearts. We desperately need Him! Can you imagine my 4-year-old telling me that he is a better driver than I am? He can't even reach the pedals! On a bigger scale, it looks even more ridiculous for us to believe that we can function independent of God and succeed.

We need God's help. In the next few chapters we will begin to discover how God works in us to produce something miraculous called *surrender*.

surrender

2 – breaking point

*"The sacrifices of God are a broken spirit;
a broken and contrite heart, O God,
you will not despise."*
Psalm 51:17

THE STRUGGLE

Mark had a fantastic family…at least, that's what everyone thought. His family was exciting, super active, and always did things together. They had great vacations, made memories, and enjoyed the fruits of his dad's hard work. They were able to drive nice cars and Mark was even able to drive a new car to school and work.

To people outside the home, it seemed like Mark had the ideal situation. His parents were generous and loved so many people. They were active in their church and his dad was a great leader for so many other men in the congregation. However, Mark felt differently about his family. People couldn't see the way his dad treated him when he "messed up" in any area of his life. In his heart, Mark felt trapped, almost as if he was not allowed to learn and grow by making mistakes. His parents seemed to expect perfection. Whenever he over-stepped boundaries, his parents would take away everything and he felt childish.

Mark began to resent his dad. He saw other people praising his dad and it only angered him more. He became frustrated when his dad would come home from work and start telling him what to do. So Mark began to stand up to his dad. He began to defy him in front of the family and argue over the smallest things that his dad told him to do. Before long, Mark began to admit that he could not wait to be on his own. He wanted to be free from the tyrant called "dad" that everyone praised and loved. He wanted to be his own man. He wanted to be...*independent.*

To his friends, Mark began to talk about his problems at home. The way he talked about it, others began to think that he really needed to be free. After all, he was 18 and almost done with high school. He should be able to make his own decisions and set his own boundaries, right? That is exactly what Mark wanted to hear. He was tired of saying "I have to ask permission from my dad" whenever people wanted to hang out or do anything fun.

Unfortunately, what Mark could not see was that the problem was not with his dad or his family. The problem was in Mark's heart. He was unwilling to love and submit to the authority God had placed in his life. Mark's problem was self-centered pride. That pride showed up in Mark's attitude, in his words, and eventually in his actions. He began to hide things from his parents because he wanted to "deal with them by himself." Little did Mark know that he was slowly destroying the greatest relationships on earth: his family.

This is a miniature version of how many Christians function in their relationship with their Creator. God calls those who believe His "children." As children of God, believers enjoy the benefits of their Heavenly Father's grace. There is limitless love and joy and peace available through that special relationship.

However, many Christians get frustrated with God's standards and God's plan. Focusing on all the restrictions and pursuits that God forbids, many Christians begin to feel "trapped" just like Mark. When God has a different plan or brings difficulty, it appears that God is a tyrant, confining, and oppressive. Looking around at the lives of others does not help. When we see other people enjoying their independence from God, it becomes easier to want that kind of life.

The fundamental problem with Mark and many Christians is the same: self-centered pride. Respect for authority dwindles away. Love for authority fades. Joy in the relationship seems like distant history and what is left is a power-struggle. Submitting to God's authority becomes more difficult and frustrating— even boring. Eventually, there is little desire for the relationship anymore.

THE BIG REVEAL

One day, Mark met with his pastor. As he began to spill out all his feelings through the tears he felt like he was understood. He had made a great case for his difficult situation and maybe his pastor would even help set his parents straight. They would finally give him the freedom and respect that he felt he needed.

The response of Mark's pastor was not what he expected. He said, "Mark, *you* are the problem." That was hard to swallow. As they talked, Mark began to see something he never had before. He began to see that it was not his dad who needed change, but rather it was his own heart. In his heart he despised authority. It had never occurred to Mark that he was valuing himself above others, and that he was seeking only to please and live for himself. What really began to open his eyes was a passage about the obedience of Jesus.

"Have this mind among yourselves, which is yours in Christ Jesus, who, though he was in the form of God, did not count equality with God a thing to be grasped, but emptied himself, by

taking the form of a servant, being born in the likeness of men. And being found in human form, he humbled himself by becoming obedient to the point of death, even death on a cross" (Phil. 2:5-8).

Jesus was obedient. Mark had never really considered the truth that Jesus was *actually obedient* in a situation that was desperate and difficult. Jesus in His humanity struggled with what would take place: His crucifixion and separation from God. But in all this, Jesus obeyed. He obeyed His Father's plan. Even though He was equal in "God-ness" to the Father, He "humbled himself by becoming obedient to the point of death" (Phil. 2:8). When Mark realized this, he broke. He understood that his desire to be equal with his dad and be independent was the attitude of Satan, not Jesus. Just like Lucifer desired to be equal with his Authority, Mark had wanted equality with his earthly authority. Just like Adam and Eve had wanted to be equal to God and be independent, Mark had wanted to be equal with his dad and be independent from him.

Mark's heart ached as he saw his disgusting rebellion and self-centeredness. He had been wrong this whole time in his view of his family and relationship with his dad. Mark's sin was now gross and shameful to him. But that was not all that troubled Mark. He saw that Jesus died for his rebellion. The pain, agony and separation from the Father that Jesus experienced on the cross was to pay the price for who Mark had been.

Oh, how we need to be at that same place as Mark! We must see that we can never be equal with our Heavenly Authority. Instead, we are nothing more than tiny creations—even our own abilities to succeed physically and spiritually are worthless.

When we crave to go the "astray way," we are actually craving to be equal with God in the authority and control of our lives. In a basic sense it is a power-struggle. Jesus paid a terrible price for the wickedness of this rebellion against God. While our hearts have been so occupied with having life our way, we have been heaping agony upon agony on the heart, soul, and body of the Savior at the cross.

APPROACHING THE PROBLEM

How do we get on board with God's plan? How do we get on the path of dependence instead of *in*dependence? This is where many Christians people mistakenly slip back into the "astray way." Here are a couple incorrect approaches:

1. *The "macho man" approach.* This is a common one. People who take this approach start adding in all kinds of really good things. It comes out in ways such as "I need to do more devotions." "I need to volunteer in more ministries." "I just need to go to

church more." They start trying to do things for God. Those are all great things. In fact, those are things that can be pleasing to God, but unfortunately, those who take this approach find themselves getting burned out.

After a few weeks it becomes too difficult to spend time in God's Word, serving becomes a drag, and life gets too crazy to make it to church consistently. When these things break down, the fight against sin feels more like trying to lift an elephant with bare hands. No one succeeds in the "macho man" approach to try harder and do better for God. The result is that people give up because they just aren't macho enough. The enemy wins again.

2. *The "super protection" approach.* This is also a common one. Those who take this approach completely rearrange life. They change their schedules, throw away their televisions, smash their iPods, and get rid of all the items they own that took time away from God or tempted them towards sin. This approach looks very admirable. They literally eliminate everything in their lives that they think pulled them away from God.

Over time, all those protections start to seem unnecessary. They start to get weary of all the "inconveniences" of their radically structured life.

They start feeling the regrets of smashing that iPod and getting rid of that 60" television. Eventually, it gets too hard to be so overprotective, and all the barriers slowly break down. With a sigh, they hop right back on the "astray way." Score another point for the enemy.

Why do those approaches always fail? Is there something wrong with doing more devotions, doing more "church," and setting up stricter standards in life? No…unless those things are the first response. The reason is that every single one of those things are external. They might seem like great things to do on the outside, but the most important part is missing. It is like telling a man who is having a heart attack to stop eating fried chicken. That is a good idea, but does not address the emergency within. (By the way, yes, you do need more devotions!) The Psalmist points us to the first response that God desires:

"For you will not delight in sacrifice, or I would give it; you will not be pleased with a burnt offering. The sacrifices of God are a broken spirit; a broken and contrite heart, O God, you will not despise" (Ps. 51:16-17).

This is exactly what God desires in us. God is not pleased by a bunch of good religious "things" as our response to Him. What pleases God, and is the first step to getting on the path of dependence, is a broken, humble heart. Those who have a broken heart are severely convicted by their sin. When they come to the realization of how *big* God is and how *small* they are in comparison, things get scary. In this moment the ugliness self-centered pride that has ruled their life is now seen with clear vision. The result is horrifying. They are able to see that their pride has really been a revolt against the Almighty God because they have been living as their own god. They have been reigning on the throne of their heart.

God wants to be on that throne. He wants to rule and reign and be recognized as the King. That is why one can do all kinds of great and godly things in order to get on the right path, but always fail. When a person is still reigning on the throne of their own heart, they will fail to turn their life around every single time.

The *only* way to approach God and get on the path of dependence is to approach Him as the King of your heart. When you approach God this way, you are finally in the right place to surrender. In our next chapter we will begin to discover how this surrender takes place.

surrender

3 – the art of surrender

"For by the grace given to me I say to everyone among you not to think of himself more highly than he ought to think, but to think with sober judgment, each according to the measure of faith that God has assigned."
Romans 12:3

BATTLE WORDS

The English word "surrender" is a word that has been used in wartime particularly in the last several hundred years. It is always a last resort. Most often, if a particular group of people are losing severely in battle, they either retreat and try to escape or they die fighting. Surrender is rather rare. It usually takes place at the very end of a war, bringing about peace and an end to all fighting. In the American Civil War, there were a series of surrenders over the course of seven months that marked the end of most war activity. General Robert E. Lee surrendered to General Ulysses S. Grant on April 9, 1865. There were surrenders of various Confederate troops throughout the next seven months, until the final surrender of the Civil War took place on November 6, 1865.

What exactly took place in those surrenders? For most, a document was signed by the surrendering party signifying that they would no longer fight and would be at the mercy of the winning side. General Lee's surrender on April 9, 1865 included a series of terms or conditions. General Lee stated that he would surrender *if* certain requests were granted and promises were made. General Grant agreed and what followed was known as a "conditional surrender." Within the terms of that surrender, all of the officers were allowed to keep their swords and side arms. The soldiers were allowed to keep their horses and mules in order to return home and use them in the upcoming season of planting and farming. This is why it was a "conditional surrender."

At the end of World War II, the Germans were given an order of "unconditional surrender." This was much different than General Lee's option in the American Civil War. The Germans would not receive any promises, exceptions or benefits other than what was declared under the international laws of war. They had to give up all weapons, all resources, and keep nothing. Everything they had they were required to give up to the Allied nations.

SURRENDER COMMANDED

Spiritually, we are at war in our own hearts. In this war we are called to an *unconditional surrender*. That means no special exceptions or special allowances. It is to be a surrender that is complete, without holding anything back. Jesus describes this surrender so well in Luke 9.

"To another he said, 'Follow me.' But he said, 'Lord, let me first go and bury my father.' And Jesus said to him, 'Leave the dead to bury their own dead. But as for you, go and proclaim the kingdom of God.' Yet another said, 'I will follow you, Lord, but let me first say farewell to those at my home.' Jesus said to him, 'No one who puts his hand to the plow and looks back is fit for the kingdom of God'" (Luke 9:59-62).

The terms for surrender to God are unconditional. We are to leave everything in life behind. Jesus is not teaching that we are to forsake our families and cut all communications with our loved ones. Rather, Jesus is teaching that in order to surrender to God and be on the path of dependence, we cannot hold on to anything else in this life. There is to be nothing that we can still claim as our own. There is to be nothing that we still value and cherish more than following Jesus. We are to literally give up our claim to everything in our lives. It means God owns us and our bodies, souls, relationships and futures. One cannot fully surrender to God while still pursuing some other dream or ambition. Jesus requires it all. Why? Because anything that we still hold on to or pursue or cherish *to keep for ourselves* is a way that we still reign on the throne of our hearts.

"No servant can serve two masters, for either he will hate the one and love the other, or he will be devoted to the one and despise the other. You cannot serve God and money" (Luke 16:13).

That is what makes surrender difficult. It is a total and complete giving up of all that we are and have...including all that we *want*.

SURRENDER GIFTED

Surrender does not begin with us making a decision. It actually starts before any of our actions or decisions take place. It is first a gift from God.

"For by the grace given to me I say to everyone among you not to think of himself more highly than he ought to think, but to think with sober judgment, each according to the measure of faith that God has assigned" (Rom. 12:3).

Surrender begins with faith that is given from God: "faith that God has assigned" (Rom. 12:3). It is not something that you and I can just go out there and "do" when we feel like it. God's work in salvation proves this.

"For by grace you have been saved through faith. And this is not your own doing; it is the gift of God" (Eph. 2:8).

Faith that is in us, moving us to surrender, is graciously *gifted* to us by God. That is why we cannot claim salvation as our own doing. If we could create our own faith, we would be able to say that it was *our* amazing ability and wisdom that turned our lives around to embrace salvation. We would not *need* God's help to have saving faith—the faith to surrender. It would mean that we could still be our own gods on the throne of our hearts. Real faith leading to surrender only comes from God.

SURRENDER AS AN ART

Talking about surrender as an *art* may at first give you the wrong impression. When phrased that way, we easily think of our own selves as the craftsmen of the art. The reality of our great God is that the opposite is true. Surrender *is* an art, but it is not our artwork. It is not our craft. It is the perfect artwork of the Perfect Craftsman. Not only is God the One Who *gifts* faith to us, but He is the One Who *grows* our faith and *moves* our faith to the place of surrender.

"…let us run with endurance the race that is set before us, looking to Jesus, the founder and perfecter of our faith…" (Heb. 12:1b-2a).

Faith is something that God is at work in the heart of a believer to perfect over a lifetime.

1. He begins with *conviction* of sin. The one who begins to experience God convicting them of their sin and wickedness is the one who God is beckoning. He is carefully opening the eyes of the heart. At this point many people make a choice to ignore God's beckoning and convicting work. This is called rebellion. Rebellion is a disgusting eruption of pride at the slightest feeling of God's touch. If we do not resist God's work of conviction, however, we begin to feel the weight of guilt. When you and I experience conviction over sin and the heaviness of guilt, we must not think we are being punished. Guilt and conviction are not punishments, but rather are beautiful, gracious works of God in our hearts.

2. God uses conviction and guilt to move us to *confession*. He uses those pressures to initiate within us our first response of confessing our sin. This is the low point. This is the place where we admit to God our ugliness and the violent disobedience of

our hearts. However, this is not the finished product. Confessing does not fix the problem. You and I know this all too well. We are familiar with confessing a sin only to return to it again and again. Confession is great in that it recognizes and agrees with God's verdict of "guilty." God is at work to do more than that.

3. As we confess our sins to the Lord and finally see a clear picture, we feel a deep sense of *grief*. Grief happens when we are *convicted*, feel the *shame* and *guilt* of our sin, *confess* our sin to God and finally *see* our situation with clarity. Paul gives us an example of this moment:

> *"Wretched man that I am! Who will deliver me from this body of death?"* (Rom. 7:24).

Grief is purposeful. When we grieve over sin, we mourn. This is only supposed to last a short time. Unfortunately, even at this point, many Christians again resist God's craftsmanship and choose to stay at the grief stage. Instead of moving ahead, the grieving stage turns into an ugly pile of self-focus and prideful pity. When this happens it is as if one says, "Stop the train, God. I'm not going any further. I want to stay here." That is a self-made trap. The trap is pride and self-pity that resists obedience and instead puts all the attention on *how I feel about what I have done.*

Many Christians choose to stay at the grief stage and swim in the pool of feelings. At the extreme, some even feel the need to grieve as a way of paying for their sins. This is not the Gospel. The Gospel in no way gives us the right or responsibility of paying for sins with guilt. Jesus paid it all. Grief is to serve a different purpose.

4. God moves us to grief only so that we can have the motivation to *repent.* That means the feelings we experience in grief are designed to push us to something further and greater.

> *"For godly grief produces a repentance that leads to salvation without regret, whereas worldly grief produces death"* (2 Cor. 7:10).

Grief is like fuel that burns in our hearts propelling us to run away from our sin and wickedness. This is why some find it so difficult to repent of sin and turn away from the "astray way." Repentance for them is nearly impossible when there is no motivation and no weight felt. They have rejected God either at the point of conviction and guilt or even confession.

When someone responds in repentance, it is only after God has done the work of convicting, bringing guilt, moving to confession and producing God-centered grief. This repentance is a turning away completely from sin and running the opposite direction. Repentance is the work of faith that God has done. That means repentance is *never* separated from faith. It is always the work of faith. God is the One Who convicts, leads us to confession and instills grief—using it to guide us to repentance.

This entire process is beautifully constructed and carried out by God. This is the work of the Perfect Craftsman. This is the art of surrender.

surrender

4 – under new management

"All mine are yours, and yours are mine,
and I am glorified in them."
John 17:10

IT WOULD TAKE A MIRACLE

In our last chapter we saw the process God brings us through in order to help us respond in repentance. It is absolutely amazing. He does such an intricate and beautiful work driving us to that place. As we saw before, repentance is like turning around and running the opposite direction. This raises a question for us. If we repent and turn the opposite direction of the "astray way," what is the new direction we are running? What is the new way? Paul gives a personal example.

"I have been crucified with Christ. It is no longer I who live, but Christ who lives in me. And the life I now live in the flesh I live by faith in the Son of God, who loved me and gave himself for me" (Gal. 2:20).

Paul's example points us directly to Christ and the Gospel. All of the work that God accomplishes in us is because of the Gospel. It is about the Gospel. It is through the Gospel. The Gospel is the truth of Christ's ultimate payment for sin and gift of restoring us to relationship with the Father. Through Adam and Eve, we all begin life running the "astray way." It is built in, but at the same time chosen by us. It is a bondage that brings with it an impossible debt. The only way for us to pay that debt is to be destroyed for a literal eternity in Hell as we saw in Chapter 1. What Jesus did was shatter the chains of our bondage to this path of sin and death by physically, emotionally and spiritually paying the debt on our behalf. When He paid that debt, He traded to us His "debtless" account of righteousness before the Father. This is the miracle of the Gospel.

That is why Paul says "I have been crucified with Christ." He is stating that all of his sin and his debt was nailed to Christ Jesus on the cross. Because of that, the perfect and holy standing Jesus had before the Father is now Paul's and ours. This is the beginning of new life. This is the foundation of the new way—the opposite of the "astray way."

GIVING IT UP

We are at a very critical point in this book. All of the chapters so far have laid out the foundation, motivation and beginnings of surrender. But that is still not the end. The final piece in all of this working of God is the actual event of surrender. We have seen in Chapter 2 that we can respond incorrectly by trying to produce change ourselves. We can also respond by rejecting God's work or being self-centered. Each of these responses chooses to either take over God's work, or refuse His work altogether.

True change only begins with God's special, miraculous craftsmanship inside us. This produces one final response in us: the giving away of ourselves. Paul illustrates what this is like. He says, "It is no longer I who live" (Gal. 2:20). That means that somewhere along the line there is a moment where we respond by completely denying ourselves and giving up everything to Jesus. It is at this moment that a person transfers all value to Jesus, all command to Jesus, all purpose to Jesus and all desires to Jesus.

That is exactly what happened in Ashley's life. As a new mom, she had begun to realize the life she always wanted was slipping away. Her dreams of traveling the world were gone. Her career as a physical therapist came to a sudden stop. She had a new baby and was stuck at home. Her husband was gone at work all week. Her friends were all happily making money and buying their first houses. While Ashley loved her baby, she hated the way her life had turned out.

Because she was so unhappy, she started to try to get some of that happiness back. Ashley felt that she had no value as a stay-at-home mom, so she started blogging. What Ashley really wanted was to feel valuable. She set up some social media accounts to interact with her blog. She began to provide instruction on topics like raising kids, fitness, gardening, shopping, DIY projects and decorating trends. Her social media accounts were loaded with pictures perfectly edited and worthy of a magazine. After a couple years Ashley had a few thousand people following her online and always commenting on her thoughtful tips on how to raise kids and have a perfect home. Ashley was driven.

Even though her efforts were successful, she wasn't as happy inside her home as she hoped. While her pictures looked awesome and her tips were far-reaching, her marriage struggled. It was difficult to respond to her husband when there was so much that she was trying to accomplish. His leadership and direction in the home sometimes conflicted with Ashley's goals. He was getting in the way. It became apparent that Ashley's life was all about Ashley. It wasn't until a friend from church gently confronted her that Ashley realized what had happened.

Her blog and social media accounts were not a sin by themselves, but her heart's desire and motivation were sinful. She had used her family and her home not as a platform to serve and love, but to promote herself. Her husband was lonely and distant. Her little girl was selfish and hateful. Ashley had made everyone slaves to her campaign of being important and trained her daughter to be just like her. So she sought counseling. As she heard the Gospel, Ashley experienced God's convicting work in her heart moving her to confession and grief over her selfish pride, and ultimately to repentance in her heart.

When all this hit her, she got down on her knees and cried out to Jesus. "God, I need Your forgiveness. I have been living completely for myself. I have craved importance and value and attention for my own pleasure. I have used my family selfishly to serve me instead of giving myself to serve them. In all of this, God, I have rejected You. I have refused to live for You. God, please take my heart. I give it to you. Take my desires and give me desires to live for You. I give You all my ambition, all my thoughts, all my feelings and my will. Please use me as a servant for Your pleasure and Your glory alone. I hold nothing back. I am Yours."

In that office on her knees Ashley surrendered. The surrender was a beautiful work of God in her heart and it completely changed her life. That wasn't just a good spiritual thing for Ashley to do. It was obedience to a command from Scripture.

"I appeal to you therefore, brothers, by the mercies of God, to present your bodies as a living sacrifice, holy and acceptable to God, which is your spiritual worship" (Rom. 12:1).

Surrender is literally a "gifting" of ourselves to God. This is produced as the final step in repentance. When you and I are driven to that step of surrender, there is a very real moment of giving back to God every part of our lives that we have been hoarding for our pleasure and desire. It means giving God the spot on the throne of our hearts. This puts us in a place of owning *nothing* about ourselves. No more living for self. No more attempting to live life for the sole purpose of bringing ourselves pleasure. This is unconditional surrender. Life now moves forward with the sole purpose of bringing pleasure to God. And the best place for this step to take place is in private prayer just like Ashley.

KEEP ON GIVING

The uniqueness of this step is that keeps on stepping. Surrender is continual. It is to be always going on, always happening, always taking place at the core of our being. Paul uses the term "living sacrifice" in Romans 12:1. Sacrifice was a very important word to the people of Israel. It was a real action that was a part of their culture and religious system. But never in the history of sacrifice was there a "living sacrifice." All sacrifices died. They were animals that were killed with their blood spilling all over an altar as a payment in exchange for sin. It was final. Every single sacrifice was given and then complete. From the moment the sacrifice ended it was a thing of the past. This new description of sacrifice is different. Instead of referring to an animal, this command of sacrifice refers to us— our lives. "Living sacrifice" is a sacrifice that stays alive. It *remains* a sacrifice. What does that mean? That means we are to *keep giving* ourselves to God as a *way of life*.

Paul speaks of this way of life as being both an inside and outside job. Rather than changing everything on the outside first, change begins within. He says it this way, "It is no longer I who live, but Christ who lives in me" (Gal. 2:20). Christ lives *in* me; this is internal. The direction we begin to go in surrender to Jesus is a direction that is totally ruled by Him, not ruled by us.

Our insides consist of a few different things: our *minds*, our *emotions* and our *wills*. These are the parts of us that *feel, think, desire* and *make decisions*. Each of them, when ruled and driven by Jesus, produce different ways of thinking, feeling, wanting and choosing than what we are used to. What is different is that each of them belongs to Jesus and depends on Jesus. This is only possible, as we have seen, through the faith that is gifted to us by God. When our inner beings (mind, desires, emotions and will) belong to Jesus and depend on Him, our lives seek something different. We begin seeking to please and bring glory to God. The effect of this inside change is that the way our lives function on the outside takes a new direction. When our minds, emotions and wills belong to God and are driven by a new desire to please Him, it also affects the way we speak, act and use our bodies.

This the same way an apple tree works. When an apple seed is planted (under the right circumstances), it takes root and sprouts into a small green plant. Over time the plant grows and bark is formed. Leaves grow as the plant gets taller and taller. Eventually, the plant is a full grown tree with roots, a trunk, branches, leaves and apples. It would be silly to try to turn an orange tree into an apple tree. If you picked off all of the oranges and then used duct tape to put apples all over the tree, it still would not be an apple tree. That is because the tree itself all the way down to the roots is still an orange tree.

Change is like this in our lives. We can't use spiritual duct tape to try and make our lives look like God-glorifiers. We need change down at the root level. It is the change at the roots of our hearts that produce God-glorifying lives on the outside. We must surrender the very core of our beings: our *hearts*.

All of this is to be a continual process for the believer. Surrender is a way of life, not a one-time event. As we surrender continually, God shows us His purposes, gives us new desires and makes us into a new kind of people that live differently. Being a living sacrifice is the way we can best worship God. Paul states that in Romans 12:1. He says "this is your spiritual worship." The question we are faced with at the end of this chapter is this: "am I surrendering everything in my heart?" If the answer is "no," what is it that you are holding on to that you cannot let yourself give away to God?

Real surrender is *unconditional*. There is nothing we are to hold back. There is to be nothing left for us to still keep and pursue for ourselves. When we surrender, all of our pursuits of pleasure, happiness and fulfillment now belong to God. If you cannot respond to God in this way, you are still on the path of independence. You are choosing the path called "the astray way."

surrender

5 – the war on independence

"Search me, O God, and know my heart!
Try me and know my thoughts! And see if there be
any grievous way in me, and lead me
in the way everlasting!"
Psalm 139:23-24

I'VE GOT THE JOY, JOY

We still have not seen the complete picture of surrender. I trust that thus far you have been able to understand just how intricately God is involved in producing this kind of faith. However, I would be giving you only a partial picture if we stopped here. There is something else that God produces in us as we surrender: unspeakable joy.

"You make known to me the path of life; in your presence there is fullness of joy; at your right hand are pleasures forevermore" (Psalm 16:11).

Joy is a gracious blessing of God. It is found in abundance when we surrender to Him. This is because surrender helps us to stop resisting God as He draws us closer to Himself. As the Psalmist said, the *fullness* of joy is found in the presence of God. It is finally here at this place of closeness to God that we experience a joy like no other. It is a precious, deep, satisfying joy that is more rich than any pleasure we get on the "astray way." Isn't that amazing? When we finally stop seeking our own pleasure and give ourselves to God for His pleasure, what we actually find is better pleasure than we have ever experienced! That is a huge encouragement for us. God did not have to bless us in this way, but by His rich, abundant grace we experience a new joy in the freedom of surrender. This satisfies our souls and fuels us to continue on as living sacrifices.

Let me illustrate how this works. Since true surrender holds nothing back, it gives away to God every part of the heart. Among those things given to God are the desires of the heart. When our sinful desires are given to God, He gives us holy and pure desires that crave Him.

"Delight yourself in the Lord, and He will give you the desires of your heart" (Psalm 37:4).

These new desires from God are good cravings. With new desires to live for God, we are fueled to seek God passionately. Here's the great part: God doesn't run away. We find Him. How do we find Him? We hear Him speak to us through His Word. We feel His Spirit at work in us convicting, guiding, comforting, channeling the Father's blessings of a special peace that gives us strength and hope. When we find God in this way, we experience the purest fulfillment of our new God-given desires.

Think about this. Instead of seeking pleasure that may never be found, through surrender God gives us deep desires that He fulfills in our hearts again and again. Wow! This causes us to echo with the Psalmist:

"Oh, taste and see that the LORD is good!" (Ps. 34:8a).

Can you imagine having desires that God loves and at the same time feeling the joy and satisfaction of those desires being met in the presence of God? This is one of the many extraordinary blessings that come from following Jesus. This joy doesn't just serve a purpose of pleasure; it serves as a weapon. Joy helps to fight a very real and dark battle in our hearts.

HELP NEEDED

Unfortunately, the moment of surrender can be short-lived. I have heard people describe this as "coming off the top of a mountain only to descend into the deepest valley." After the new feelings of joy and freedom fade, we can start to feel something old creeping back into our hearts. It is the urge to be independent. If left unchecked, we can easily go back to the familiar urges in our hearts and begin to obey them. This is the war waging inside every believer. We will refer to it as "the war on independence". This is a common war that was waged even in the heart of Paul.

"So I find it to be a law that when I want to do right, evil lies close at hand. For I delight in the law of God, in my inner being, but I see in my members another law waging war against the law of my mind and making me captive to the law of sin that dwells in my members" (Rom. 7:21-23).

Here's what Paul is referring to. For believers, there are two different kinds of desires in our hearts: old desires for independence and new, pure desires from God. These are both at odds and create conflict within. It is what keeps our hearts from being completely trustworthy. Like the danger in the advice I received in Chapter 1 to follow my heart, it is not safe to just do what I feel. I can't trust my heart completely, because there are dangerous urges inside.

The good news is that there is a way to fight against the urge to be independent. In a basic way, we are to fight *independence* with *dependence*. The book of Psalms is loaded with expressions of dependence and humility. One in particular stands out as a weapon.

"Search me, O God, and know my heart! Try me and know my thoughts! And see if there be any grievous way in me, and lead me in the way everlasting!" (Ps. 139:23-24).

In order to fight against the independence of our hearts we need help. That's why the first cry of the Psalmist we just read recognized God's power and authority. It is God's power and God's authority that demand our allegiance and our dependence. The problem we face in our "independence cravings" is a problem of self-worth and self-ability. In a way, we can gradually think of ourselves as equal with God. When this happens we believe that somehow we have the ability and wisdom to guide ourselves to lasting pleasure apart from God's help. That is incredibly dangerous, but many Christians live this way. The truth is, we will never be dependent on God if we believe that we are equal with Him.

How does this show up? It shows up in our behavior (seeking our own way), in our attitudes (feeling like we can handle life), and in our communication (talking about our lives and experiences to promote our abilities and wisdom). The Psalmist had a different approach. He first asks God for help! He cries out to God about something very personal: his heart. He recognizes that he needs help on the inside.

This shows us that the battle against independence must be faced head-on in the heart. In our hearts we face the temptation to turn back to the "astray way"—the way of independence. Recognizing this inside warfare, the Psalmist begins with a plea for God to search his heart. That means he is asking God to find any place where he has drifted back to independence. There is a goal in mind. He is not just asking God to point out error, he is asking God to lead him in the way he should go. At the bottom line of all of this is *dependence*. This must be our goal.

There is a sense in which some Christians stop half-way. Rather than seeking to depend on God and follow His leading, they simply want God to help point out a few errors. That is like saying, "Hey, God, please show me where I am messing up. Ok, thanks for that, I've got it from here." We must not approach God that way. We need more than God's observation; we need His guidance! When we seek God's help, we must seek it with an eager heart to follow Him in obedience.

REPAIR REQUIRED

One of the many ways that God guides us and shows us how to obey is through His Word. How do you view the Bible? Do you see it as dry sand to sift through, or do you see it as a well of Pure Water that can quench your greatest thirst? Your view of God's Word will determine how you approach it. In the war on independence, God's Word is of the highest importance for us. We can see that through Paul's instruction immediately following the command to be "living sacrifices."

"Do not be conformed to this world, but be transformed by the renewal of your mind, that by testing you may discern what is the will of God, what is good and acceptable and perfect" (Rom. 12:2).

In order to keep from going back to the "astray way" (conforming to this world), Paul says to be "transformed by the renewal of your mind" (Rom. 12:2). What does that mean? Am I supposed to just go out there and try to keep my mind in healthy spiritual shape? No. Being renewed in our minds is not about us fixing ourselves, but instead going into the Divine Workshop where God operates on us through His Word.

"But that is not the way you learned Christ!—assuming that you have heard about him and were taught in him, as the truth is in Jesus, to put off your old self, which belongs to your former manner of life and is corrupt through deceitful desires, and to be renewed in the spirit of your minds" (Eph. 4:20-23).

"Be renewed in the spirit of your minds." Not only do our hearts need help, but our minds are in need of transformation. To be specific, there are things *within* our minds that need to be fixed. The part that needs fixing is the constant mindset you and I fall back into—a mind that places self at the center of life, exalting and lifting self to the position of being king.

How do we renew that mind? It is renewed by constantly feasting on God's Word. As we feast we are reminded of our place as servants of the great King Jesus. We are reminded of the Gospel. God uses His Word to return us to the perspective we had at the cross. Ultimately, God uses His Word to accomplish in us the work of conviction, guilt, confession, grief, repentance and surrender. This is exactly what we need! Our minds are renewed to think clearly as children of God, not slaves to our former cravings. I have heard some Christians say that they do not need to read God's Word because they "already understand and know what His Word says." They no longer see a need to constantly feast on Scripture. That is so dangerous! How are we to be confronted with the right perspective if we refuse to have our minds renewed in Scripture?

My brother's truck reminds me of this. When he went off to college, I drove his blue 1988 Chevy Silverado for over a year. I knew that the engine needed oil, but I didn't want to take the time to go to the repair shop and get an oil change. I decided that I would just throw in a little oil every few months. I didn't really want to take it to a shop. I thought I knew better. What I didn't realize was that the old oil turned to a dirt-filled slime and was beginning to destroy the engine. Finally, the truck died; I had murdered the engine. What I should have done was take it to the repair shop to get the oil renewed on a regular basis. If I had done that, the old oil would have been purged and the new oil would have been able to do its proper work.

It works the same way with Scripture. We must go to the Divine Workshop to have our minds renewed regularly in God's Word. If we refuse to do this, our thinking slowly gets polluted. Eventually our polluted thinking causes us to stop depending on God and our lives become consumed with sinful pride. This kills surrender. It causes us to back-track and seek the path of independence.

This spiritual war is real. It threatens to cut off our allegiance to God. It threatens to put a stop to our lives being living sacrifices. We must seek God's help rooting out our sin and seek guidance through His Word to renew our minds, producing obedience.

So where are you? Have you been refusing to seek God's help identifying your sin? Have you neglected to seek God's leading away from self-centered perspectives, desires and habits? Is your thinking polluted because you have ignored the need to have your mind renewed? If so, please do not continue responding with a cry for independence. Will you stop right now and humbly plead with God as the Psalmist did?

"Search me, O God, and know my heart! Try me and know my thoughts! And see if there be any grievous way in me, and lead me in the way everlasting!" (Ps. 139:23-24).

Enlist in the war on independence by seeking God's help and guidance. Be ready to obey. The war is ferocious, but winning is something our great King specializes in. He can have victory in your heart and in your mind. If you are in the middle of that battle, don't grow weary. Remember, on the other side of surrender is a joy and pleasure too deep for words to describe.

6 – a warning

"I tell you, this man went down to his house justified,
rather than the other. For everyone who exalts himself
will be humbled, but the one who humbles himself
will be exalted."
Luke 18:14

FAKE OUT

The Hague Convention of 1907 specifically states, "It is especially forbidden to make improper use of a flag of truce." In other words, you cannot fake surrender. This was a dirty tactic that had been used in many instances throughout history. It would happen when a particular war party signaled a "truce." As soon as the enemy approached with lowered weapons they would attack and kill them. Their intention was never to surrender, but instead to trick the other party into believing they surrendered so that they could continue on in their pursuit of victory.

At our current phase in history, false surrender is prohibited by the international laws of war.

Interestingly, earthly war is not the only place that false surrender happens. We also see something about it in Scripture: a spiritual warning.

"He also told this parable to some who trusted in themselves that they were righteous, and treated others with contempt: 'Two men went up into the temple to pray, one a Pharisee and the other a tax collector. The Pharisee, standing by himself, prayed thus: 'God, I thank you that I am not like other men, extortioners, unjust, adulterers, or even like this tax collector. I fast twice a week; I give tithes of all that I get.' But the tax collector, standing far off, would not even lift up his eyes to heaven, but beat his breast, saying, 'God, be merciful to me, a sinner!' I tell you, this man went down to his house justified, rather than the other. For everyone who exalts himself will be humbled, but the one who humbles himself will be exalted'" (Luke 18:9-14).

Jesus gives an amazing story of two men praying. Both of them appeared to be in "surrender" to God. Although the first one was very clean on the outside, he had no intention of living for God's pleasure. It may have looked like that to others, but it was a fake surrender. His speech shows us exactly what condition his heart was in. What this man had was a heart consumed with selfish pride. His heart was not broken. He was not humble. In all this he wanted to please himself by trying to look better than everyone. If he looked better than everyone, people would think the highest of him. Perhaps even God would think best of him. It was a selfish, consuming mindset. Ultimately, it meant that he never really surrendered in his heart.

The second man, on the other hand, was in the midst of true surrender. He was going through the process of conviction, guilt, confession, grief and repentance.

I want us to focus on the first man. Everything he did seemed to be an evidence of surrender on the outside. Look at how he appears to be on fire for God. He fasts *twice* a week for God? Wow, he must really have a great prayer life. He tithes consistently from *everything* he gets paid? Wow, he must really trust God with his finances. Do you see how easy it would be for us to think that this guy is a super-Christian? It would be very easy. On the inside, however, he had no intention of being broken and humble. His heart's intention was to bring himself pleasure by getting everyone—including God—to think highly of him. Really he only cared about himself. That's fake surrender.

Fake surrender is giving up things in your life to God in order to look better. What that means is that you don't end up surrendering what's on the inside. You only surrender what people can see, but at the same time live as the ruler on the throne of your own heart. Beware of this. Half surrender does not bring you the pleasure that you might think. It cuts you off from getting rich, satisfying pleasure and joy in the presence of God.

There are two specific motivations I want to warn you of when it comes to surrender. Beware of surrendering for the sake of your *reputation.* Do not be mistaken. This is easy for all of us to do. I remember going to a summer camp growing up where I fell into this trap. At the end of the week the entire camp of around a thousand people would get in line to throw a stick into a fire. This stick, we were told, symbolized our lives. We were called to throw that stick into the fire as a sign of surrendering our entire lives to God. Like cattle, almost everyone in the room took part in the ritual sacrifice.

What was wrong was that there were many who were unwilling to surrender their hearts to the rule of King Jesus, but cared much about what others thought. It was easy to get in line, start crying, grab that stick and slowly drop it into the fire marking yourself as one of the "surrendered ones."

Now, I don't want to bash everyone there. There really were people that were genuine. I remember times that I felt so ashamed of my unwillingness to surrender to God that I reached a breaking point at that final service. There were times God worked in my heart in that place. However, I am ashamed to admit, there were times when I got in line and threw a stick into the fire because I wanted my youth pastor to see me as a better person. The result was pretend surrender. It had nothing to do with pleasing God. It was all about me trying to gain approval and praise. Beware of this. It can be easy to look "surrendered" on the outside in order to promote yourself. Pretend surrender is not real surrender.

There is a second warning about false surrender. Beware of surrendering for the sake of God owing you some kind of *reward*. I am reminded of this by the attitude of the disciples at one particular point in Jesus' ministry.

"Then Peter said in reply, 'See, we have left everything and followed you. What then will we have?'" (Matt. 19:27).

Peter spoke for all the disciples when he expressed this concern to Jesus. He refers to the extent of the disciples' surrender. They left everything they had and everything they were living for to follow Jesus. The problem was many of them had a wrong motivation. They were hoping for an earthly kingdom. The disciples really believed that Jesus was going to set up a kingdom in Jerusalem and finally free them from the control of the Roman government.

At this point, they failed to see the spiritual victory that Jesus was accomplishing. Jesus did not come to establish an earthly victory, but instead a spiritual victory. Peter was asking Jesus "What's in it for us?" He believed that there was some kind of special reward for surrendering to Jesus and following Him. The disciples all thought this way. In fact, they argued often about who was going to get the biggest reward in the earthly kingdom they thought was about to begin. They wanted to be rewarded with the right-hand seat next to Jesus when He became King.

Now it can be easy to look at the disciples and think that they were just being foolish. However, if we are honest, we fall into that same trap. Many Christians surrender to God thinking that God is going to improve all of their circumstances. Jesus never promised that. All of the rewards Jesus promised for those who would follow Him were spiritual blessings. Many of those were in reference to a future kingdom after this earthly life. Do not seek earthly reward for spiritual surrender. It is a selfish motivation. It is a *conditional* surrender, because there is still pride ruling in the heart that seeks pleasure through selfish ambition. Beware of this in your heart.

Both of these motivations are false surrenders. When our motivations to surrender are all about our reputation improving or the rewards that we think God will owe us, we are not really surrendering *everything*. True surrender begins with brokenness, not selfish ambition. It gives everything to God for His pleasure instead of our pleasure in some kind of reward.

God is not fooled by fake, pretend, half-hearted, conditional, or even convenient surrender. It is painful for Him. Jesus uncovered hypocrisy and false surrender all throughout His earthly ministry.

"You hypocrites! Well did Isaiah prophesy of you, when he said: 'This people honors me with their lips, but their heart is far from me'" (Matt. 15:7-8).

Real surrender is not an outside act, but an inside revolution. Do not fall into a self-centered trap. Heed the warning. If you are at a place of surrender, simply ask yourself, "Why am I surrendering? What is my motivation?" We are called to surrender—to give ourselves completely away to God—because He is the rightful owner of us. He created and paid for us through Jesus' sacrifice. If you are motivated to surrender for any other reason than obedience to God out of love and worship, chances are that you are being motivated to a fake surrender.

surrender

closing thoughts

I trust you have been able to get a clear picture of how surrender works. The hard part about a book like this is that there is no prayer to pray at the end. There is no set of special words for me to give you enabling you to surrender fully to God. That is on purpose. I am so glad there is no magical prayer to give you. That would not be real surrender. As we have seen, real surrender is a work of God. Your responsibility is in your response. How will you respond to God's work in your heart? Will you give everything? Or will you choose to believe it is better to hold on to that one thing in your life you love so much. I hope not. I hope and pray that God's knocking at the door of your heart will be so loud that you cannot resist anymore.

If you don't know Jesus—if you have never been at the place of repentance and surrender—what is holding you back? Does the idea of dependence scare you or seem completely unnecessary? I'm praying that

God works in you to respond in faith—a faith that gives away your heart, your body, your relationships, your ambitions, your plans, your habits, your preferences, your feelings, your desires, your decisions, your stuff, your fears, your family, your future—*your life.*

If you do know Jesus, are you presenting yourself to God as a living sacrifice? Or have you been too eager to get back on the "astray way"? Surrender to God. Give Him everything. And then joyfully pursue a life of obedience and dependence on the very God Who created and purchased you with His own literal blood. The truth is we are all in need of God's continued work to accomplish in our hearts the art of surrender. Let's respond to that work with a humble "yes," and experience the victory found only by the faithful hand of our faithful King. To God be the glory!

"So then, brothers, we are debtors, not to the flesh, to live according to the flesh. For if you live according to the flesh you will die, but if by the Spirit you put to death the deeds of the body, you will live. For all who are led by the Spirit of God are sons of God. For you did not receive the spirit of slavery to fall back into fear, but you have received the Spirit of adoption as sons, by whom we cry, 'Abba! Father!'" (Rom. 8:12-15).

surrender

ABOUT THE AUTHOR

Michael Summers has a passion for shepherding youth. He holds a degree in Pastoral Studies from Northland International University and has led student ministry at Countryside Baptist Church in Olathe, KS since 2010. What Michael is most excited about is seeing students surrender their hearts to Christ and be discipled in the truth of God's Word. He has been married to Kimberly since 2008 and loves being a father to their son Thomas and daughter Mary. They are expecting their next child, Michael Remington, to arrive around the month of August 2016.

surrender

surrender

33834409R00049

Made in the USA
Middletown, DE
29 July 2016